IMAGES

Food

Karen Bryant-Mole

First published in Great Britain by Heinemann Library, Halley Court, Jordan Hill, Oxford OX2 8EJ,
a division of Reed Educational & Professional Publishing Ltd.

OXFORD FLORENCE PRAGUE MADRID ATHENS MELBOURNE AUCKLAND KUALA LUMPUR
SINGAPORE TOKYO IBADAN NAIROBI KAMPALA JOHANNESBURG GABORONE
PORTSMOUTH NH (USA) CHICAGO MEXICO CITY SAO PAULO

Designed by Jean Wheeler
Commissioned photography by Zul Mukhida
Produced by Mandarin Offset Ltd.
Printed and bound in China

01 00 99 98 97
10 9 8 7 6 5 4 3 2 1

ISBN 0 431 06310 9

British Library Cataloguing in Publication Data
Bryant-Mole, Karen
Food. - (Images)
1.Food - Juvenile literature 2. Readers (Primary)
I.Title
641.3

**Some of the more difficult words in this book are
explained in the glossary.**

Acknowledgements
The Publishers would like to thank the following for permission to reproduce photographs. Cephas; 4 (right) Mick Rock,
17 (left), Chapel Studios; 16 (right) Zul Mukhida, Tony Stone Images; 4 (left) Andy Sacks,
5 (right) Annette Soumillard, 16 (left) Laurie Evans, 17 (right) Paul Webster, Zefa; 5 (left).

Every effort has been made to contact copyright holders of any material reproduced in this book. Any omissions will be
rectified in subsequent printings if notice is given to the Publisher.

Contents

Farms

Most of the food we eat comes from farms.

fruit

cereals

Different farms produce different types of food.

meat

vegetables

Vegetables

There are lots of different types of food.

These are all
vegetables.

7

Fruit

What is your favourite fruit?

bananas

plums

peaches

strawberries

oranges

9

Milk

Foods made from milk are called dairy **products**.

milk

cheese

cream

yoghurt

butter

Cooking

Some food has to be cooked
before we can eat it.
Some food can be eaten **raw**.

Which of these foods
are usually cooked?

Ingredients

When these things are mixed together and cooked, they will make a cake.

14

They are called the ingredients
of the cake.

Around the world

The **recipes** for these meals come from different parts of the world.

pizza from Italy

sushi from Japan

curry from India

noodles from
China

Food for growth

Different foods help our bodies in different ways.

These foods help our bodies to grow.

19

Food for energy

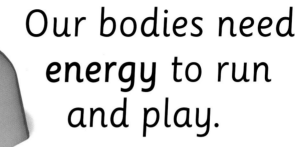

Our bodies need **energy** to run and play.

These foods are good at giving our bodies energy.

21

Keeping healthy

Eating too much sugar or fat is not good for our bodies.

Eating a variety of food helps to keep our bodies healthy.

23

Glossary

cereals   special grasses with seeds that can be
  eaten e.g. wheat, maize, barley, rice, oats and rye
energy   what makes things (including people)
  go or work
products   things that are made
raw   not cooked
recipes   instructions that tell people how to make
meals, cakes or other food dishes

Index

24